Skateboarding

Skateboarding

Mike Kennedy

SCHOLASTIC INC.

New York Toronto London Auckland Sydney
Mexico City New Delhi Hong Kong Buenos Aires

Note to readers: Definitions for words in **bold** can be found in the Glossary at the back of this book.

The cover image shows a skateboarder skating up a half-pipe in Boulder, Colorado. The image opposite the title page shows John Stephenson skateboarding in Marina Del Rey, California.

Copyright © 2003, 2001 by Franklin Watts, a division of Scholastic Inc.
All rights reserved. Published by Scholastic Inc., 557 Broadway, New York, NY 10012.
Printed in the U.S.A.

ISBN 0-531-18673-3

SCHOLASTIC and associated logos and designs are trademarks and/or registered trademarks of Scholastic Inc.

1 2 3 4 5 6 7 8 9 10   61   12 11 10 09 08 07 06 05 04 03

Contents

Skateboarding developed in California when bored surfers began looking for new thrills.

Chapter One

Roll With It

Some people say, "Necessity is the mother of invention." It means that a growing need for something can give birth to new ideas. That is how the skateboard came to be. It was invented in the 1950s for surfers who wanted a way to ride waves when the sea was calm.

Thousands of years ago, quiet seas were the least of anyone's worries! Around 5500 B.C., the people of Mesopotamia had a problem. They used giant stone blocks to build palaces. They also used them to make monuments. They realized they needed a better way to move the heavy blocks. At first, they made a new tool called a sledge. (A sledge is a platform that lets workers drag heavy loads along the ground. It is sort of like a skateboard without wheels.) It was better than nothing. But it was still very heavy. Next, they found that laying a bunch of logs under the sledge helped it roll along. But the blocks were not much easier to move.

Fast forward 2,000 years. The Mesopotamians came up with a new idea. They sliced narrow pieces from the ends of the logs. They stuck them to the side of the sledge. They did not need the heavy logs anymore. The wheel was born!

Sidewalk Surfing

Time to fast forward again. More than 5,000 years passed before the first skateboard rolled onto the scene. It's not that people weren't trying. Inventors were always coming up with clever uses for the wheel. Wheels gave people speed! By 1850, bicycles and roller skates had been invented in different parts of the world. Biking and skating soon became popular sports. That is, until the car engine came along. After that, adults lost interest in bikes and skates. But kids still lived to ride! They kept the flame alive.

By 1900, kids had begun to build their own scooters. All it took was a wood plank, a fruit crate, and a pair of old roller skates. This hobby was pretty big in California. So was another new fad—surfing.

When the waves were right for surfing, everyone headed for the beach. But when the Pacific Ocean was calm, it was a

SPRINGFIELD BICYCLE CLUB.

BICYCLE CAMP-EXHIBITION & TOURNAMENT.
SPRINGFIELD, MASS. U.S.A. SEPT. 18.19.20. 1883.

real drag. By the 1950s, surfers were asking themselves an interesting question. Was there a way to surf on dry land? Where there's a will, there's a way! And so they found a way to surf on the ground. All they had to do was attach roller skates to their boards. Those were the first skateboards!

Cycling and skating became popular sports in the 1800s, as shown by this poster advertising a cycling event in 1883.

9

Who Invented the Skateboard?

No one knows for sure. But many credit Bill Richards. He was raised in California in the 1920s. In some ways, Bill never really grew up. Even as an adult, he loved the feeling of the wind rushing through his hair. He loved surfing. He and his son, Mark, ran a surf shop in California. They had many customers who came in all the time. They were hooked on the excitement of surfing.

One day in 1958, Bill and Mark thought up a cool idea. They could keep surfers busy even when there were no waves. Father and son sawed off a piece of wood. Then they attached the wheels from some roller skates. Their new invention seemed like it might be fun. So they displayed it in their shop. Many people say that the Richards' made the first skateboard.

By 1960, surf shops all over California were selling skateboards. At first, this new craze was called sidewalk surfing. But soon everyone just called it "skateboarding." They got the name from the boards themselves. Surf shops everywhere built and sold their own skateboards. Toy companies did the same. The skateboard quickly developed into a fad. Everybody had to own one.

A man named Larry Stevenson was good at promoting new ideas. He thought skateboarding could get even bigger. His instinct told him to start his own skateboard company. He started Makaha Skateboards. In 1963, he decided to sponsor a skateboard event. Skateboarders could come and show off their greatest stunts. When word spread, everyone wanted to buy tickets to come. It was a huge success. The next year, Larry called the event the National Skateboard Championships. People across the nation tuned in to watch the contest on TV.

Larry Stevenson (left), founder of one of the first skateboarding companies, helps a skater perform a handstand on his skateboard.

No Pip Squeak

Brad "Squeak" Blank won Larry Stevenson's first skateboarding contest in 1963.

11

This photo from 1965 shows teenagers practicing their balance as they skate down the sidewalk.

At about the same time, another young Californian named Hobie Alter started his own company. Hobie's skateboards were just as good as Makaha's. The two began a friendly competition to see who could make the best boards. They tried lighter and more flexible materials. They got rid of the steel wheels. Wheels made of fired clay were faster. They made better **trucks** and **axles** to attach the wheels to the board.

Better skateboards made the sport even more popular. Kids rode on boards everywhere. They rode in driveways. They rode in schoolyards. They rode on city streets. But their favorite place to ride was swimming pools—without the water!

There were no bumps, so the ride was always smooth.

Around this time, some American riders became big stars. John Freis, Torger Johnson, Phil Edwards, and Dave Hilton were the best in the sport. They launched themselves off of special ramps. They spun in the air. They did handstands on their boards. Crowds watched, amazed.

How were skateboarders able to keep their balance? Why didn't they fall and get hurt? The truth is that many did. In 1965, the American Medical Association said that skateboards were a "medical **menace**." That scared a lot of people. The sport grew less popular. By 1967, most parents would not let their children own skateboards. The sport nearly died.

A Nas-Worthy Idea

Frank Nasworthy realized why skateboarders crashed so often. As a rider, he knew clay wheels didn't grip the road well. One day in 1971, a friend told him about a tough material called urethane. Frank liked to invent things. He wondered if urethane might work for skateboard wheels. After making a set, he saw two things right away. The wheels rolled more smoothly than clay ones. And, they did not slip and slide.

Frank was very excited. He showed his discovery to friends. He then started a company making his new wheels. Almost overnight, skateboarding was reborn. Thanks to urethane wheels, the sport was safer. It was also more fun. New skateboard companies popped up everywhere. Different versions of the sport gained popularity as well. People skateboarded down steep hills. They went around obstacles. They made up tricks. A good imagination was a skateboarder's best friend.

At this point, the hardest part about skateboarding was finding a place to practice. Skateboarders needed wide open spaces. They needed smooth surfaces. That's when skateboard parks began to appear. The first park opened in Florida in 1976. It looked like the bottom of a huge swimming pool, with ramps and curves everywhere. For a small fee, skateboarders could ride all day long. The idea was an instant success. Parks opened by the hundreds in the following months. From these

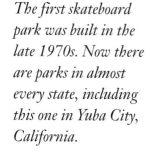

The first skateboard park was built in the late 1970s. Now there are parks in almost every state, including this one in Yuba City, California.

skateboard parks came a wave of young and fearless riders. Rodney Mullen became a **freestyle** champion at age thirteen. Russ Howell added twists and leaps to the sport. Laura Thornhill was one of the first girls to become a star.

A rider named Willi Winkel also made his mark. He invented the **half-pipe** in 1977. In skateboarding's early days, it was hard to get going really fast. The quarter-pipe helped. It was a ramp shaped like half of the letter U, and it was used in the early 1970s. This ramp let skateboarders pick up speed just by rolling down off a raised platform. But sometimes Willi would do just the opposite. He would gather speed on a flat

surface. Then he would go up a quarter-pipe. And then he would soar in the air for a moment. Looking at a quarter-pipe one day, he had a brainstorm. Why not move two quarter-pipes together to form a U-shaped ramp? The results were amazing. After charging down one side, Willi was able to roar back up the other. This let him fly even higher.

Soon, riders everywhere learned about the half-pipe. They made models of their own. The pipes opened the door to a whole new world of stunts. But they also

Skateboarder Blaze Blouin performs on the half-pipe at the Pro-Am Championships in Anaheim, California.

created a whole new set of problems. Sparked by the thrill of catching air, riders got fierce. They grew brave. And they got more tricky. So the risk of getting hurt grew greater as well. This made it very expensive to run skateboard parks. Families often sued the parks when their kids got hurt. Many parks went out of business. By 1979, for the second time, the future of skateboarding looked shaky.

16

Hardcore Comeback

In the early 1980s, a small group of skateboarding fans remained. But they refused to let their sport die. With fewer skate parks open, riders went back to the streets and schoolyards. They kept up with the skateboard scene by reading skateboarding magazines. At the same time, the National Skateboard Association was busy holding contests across the country. Clothing companies created light shoes that hugged the boards. They made hip clothing just for riders.

Hardcore riders, including a youngster named Tony Hawk, loved skateboarding's cool fashions and rebellious lifestyle. In 1979, at age eleven, Tony told his father that he was giving up all sports but skateboarding. Three years later, he was crowned national champion. His rise to fame sparked new interest in the sport.

By the mid-1980s, skateboarding had started to enter the **mainstream**. More than 11 million people in the United States had tried the sport, including actor Michael J. Fox. In *Back to the Future*, his character, Marty McFly, was shown "inventing" the skateboard. In the film's sequel, Fox rode a

Out-Foxed

After watching *Back to the Future*, you might think Michael J. Fox is an expert skateboarder. That is not entirely true. In the movie, professional riders Bob Schmelzer and Per Welinder performed his most daring stunts. This was certainly lucky for Fox. He once said that he would probably crash if he tried any tricks that hard.

In the movie Back to the Future 2, *Michael J. Fox races to safety on his hover board, a futuristic version of the skateboard.*

space-age version of a skateboard. It had no wheels and was called a hover board.

Today, skateboarding is no longer just a fad. Companies from around the globe are still trying to improve boards. They also have advanced safety equipment. Falling still hurts. But it no longer means an automatic trip to the emergency room. Riders are always working on amazing new stunts. Skate parks are again opening in every state. Skateboarding contests include exciting events such as the Gravity Games and the X Games. The sport is the subject of hundreds of Web sites. True, skateboarding might not have been an overnight hit. But centuries after the wheel was invented and forty years after Californians began **shredding** on homemade boards, the sport has proven that it's here to stay!

Skateboarders can perform a variety of stunts and tricks with their skateboards.

Chapter Two

Rad Stunts and Tricks

Why do people like skateboarding so much? Some like zooming up the half-pipe and flying off the **lip**. Some like performing in front of crowds. Some simply like the cool clothes skateboarders wear. Best of all, skateboarders like to let their imaginations run wild. This is how all the best tricks are invented. First, they picture a new stunt in their mind's eye. Then, they practice it again and again until it's perfect.

Better Boards, Better Tricks

In the old days, skateboarders were held back by their equipment. They wanted to try different stunts, but their boards would not let them. The first skateboards were much heavier and stiffer than today's models. So it was hard for a rider to do anything really tough. All that changed thanks to several major breakthroughs.

The kicktail is the back end of the deck that turns up toward the sky. Many of today's boards have kicktails on both ends.

Fiberglass changed everything. Larry Gordon brought this material to the sport in 1964. He owned a company that made surfboards. But he was also interested in skateboarding. At that time, everyone used wood to make the **deck** of a skateboard. Larry knew that fiberglass was less stiff. He soon realized that by mixing fiberglass and wood he could build a better skateboard. The result of his work was a deck that bent but did not break. Riders loved Larry's new skateboard. It moved like it was attached to the bottom of their feet.

Another important invention was the **kicktail**. It came late in the 1960s. The kicktail lets skateboarders lean back and roll on their rear wheels. Of course, the introduction of urethane wheels was also key. They gave the smoothest ride yet. A smooth ride makes it easier to balance. It also allows skateboarders to try more difficult tricks.

A New Bag of Tricks

By the late 1970s, skateboard companies were making much better boards. As you might guess, this is when many of today's cool stunts were invented. Before that, riders mostly copied the moves from surfing. Now, they began to develop special styles of their own. A new move called the **Ollie** was the greatest trick of them all.

Before the invention of the half-pipe, riders were limited by the laws of gravity because rising off the ground was difficult. This helped keep skateboarding at a standstill. Then along came a kid named Alan "Ollie" Gelfand. One day in 1977, he began fooling around with a new move. As Gelfand sped up one side of a half-pipe, he shifted his weight back and pressed his right foot on his board's kicktail. The move shot him and his skateboard into the air—and right onto his rear end! After trying the move a few more times, he was

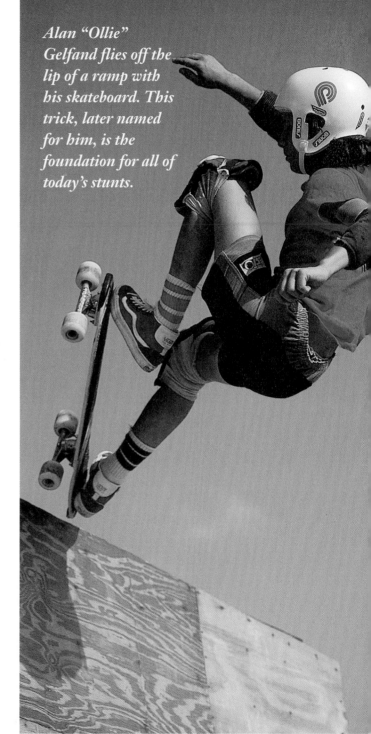

Alan "Ollie" Gelfand flies off the lip of a ramp with his skateboard. This trick, later named for him, is the foundation for all of today's stunts.

able to land safely. Skateboarding had taken to the skies. The trick became known as the Ollie in his honor.

News of the Ollie spread quickly through the skateboarding world. Gelfand was put on the cover of a skateboarding magazine. He showed other riders how to do his move. They put their own spins on it. Mark Gonzalez was the first to rise onto hand rails. Jeff Phillips created the "Phillips 66." Duane Peters, known as the "Master of Disaster," thrilled crowds with the "loop of life." Mike McGill made a name for himself with the "McTwist." He spun backwards on his board one and a half turns in the air. It seemed that somebody added a new twist to the Ollie every day. In fact, riders still dream up funny names for their best tricks. This makes the sport fun. And it is another way for skateboarders to be creative.

Getting Technical

Today, skateboarding needs more than a good imagination. The sport has become highly technical. Serious skateboarders practice all the time. They leave nothing to chance. They rely on pinpoint accuracy. They need full confidence to complete all their stunts during contests.

Skateboarders know that they owe a lot to Alan Gelfand. This is because the Ollie remains the basis for nearly every stunt invented. When Bob Burnquist performs his "Burntwist," he is doing an Ollie. When Chet Thomas rises on a park bench, he is doing an Ollie. When you see a picture of Daewon Song soaring through the air, he is doing an Ollie. As Tony Hawk says, "Almost every trick starts with an Ollie." How far can the Ollie be taken? The sky may be the only limit.

Skateboarding stunts are highly technical and require lots of practice.

The crowded stands at the 1999 X Games in San Francisco are a tribute to the rising popularity of skateboarding.

Chapter Three

Lights, Camera, Action

Skateboarding was not always popular. Back when the sport first got started, only a small number of people were interested in it. Competitions were not shown on television, and it was hard to find magazines that covered skateboarding. Few people took the sport seriously. They believed that riders would soon get bored with it.

To make matters worse, some skateboarders had reputations as bad kids. They didn't always follow the rules in school and at home. This gave critics even more reason to hope the sport would die. Of course, skateboarding did not die. Today it has a following worldwide.

Coming Attractions

There were early signs that skateboarding might be more than a fad. In 1965, *The Quarterly Skateboarder*, the first magazine devoted to the sport, hit the newsstands. In May of the same

This 1965 photo of kids showing off on their skateboards shows why some people hoped the sport's popularity would fade.

year, *Life* magazine ran a photo of Pat McGee on its cover. She was the girls' national skateboarding champion. The story inside looked at "the craze and the menace of skateboards."

Around the same time, Hollywood made the first movie about skateboarding. *Skater Dater* looked at the problem of peer pressure among teenagers. Jan and Dean, a popular singing group, put out a song called "Sidewalk Surfing." The organizers of the National Skateboard Championships in California were also singing a happy tune. Suddenly, their event had become a national craze.

A Healthy Thrash

During the 1970s, skateboarders turned away from the surfer image. In fact, they did not care what people thought of them. Some riders were rebels. Many had wild haircuts. They wore messy clothes. They felt that no one was ever going to treat skateboarding as a real sport. Little did they know, people were starting to change their minds.

Many riders had a "Who cares?" attitude. But the sport was getting more popular. By 1975, contests were popping up all over the world. More movies were being made about skateboarding. One was called *Skateboard*. It starred a teenager named Leif Garrett. He was already a pop star when the movie came out in 1978. Movie critics said that the skateboarding scenes were the best part.

This kind of attention was great for the sport. Pros Tony Alva and Ellen Oneal did all of the movie's tough stunts. As a

Press Clippings

In 1977, articles on skateboarding began to appear in *Sports Illustrated*.

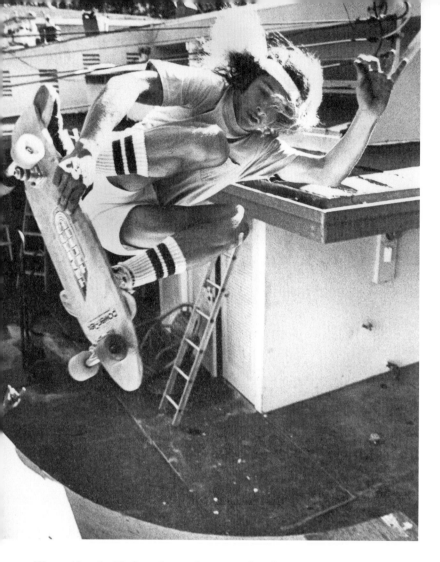

Tony Alva is 12 feet above the ground as he soars through the air during this stunt. His skateboarding talents were used in the 1978 movie Skateboard.

movie, *Skateboard* was a dud. But it was a great advertisement for skateboarding. People loved watching all the amazing stunts.

These top skateboarders fueled the sport in the early 1980s. They gained a voice in 1981, when *Thrasher* magazine came out. *Thrasher* took the sport from the streets to the newsstands.

The Big Time

During the 1980s and 1990s, other magazines came out. Some are still around today. Each gives a different perspective on

Roll the Cameras

Skateboarding has been featured in plenty of movies, including *Spinnin' Wheels* (1975), *Five Summer Stories—Plus Four* (1975), *Super Session* (1976), *Freewheelin'* (1976), *Hard Waves/Soft Wheels* (1977), and *Police Academy 4: Citizens on Patrol* (1987).

skateboarding. *TransWorld Skateboarding* offers beautiful pictures of wild new tricks. *Heckler* looks at all levels of the sport. *Skateboarder* is aimed at young riders.

The magazine rack is not the only place to learn about skateboarding. Your local video store may have two movies for rent. One, called *Thrashin'*, shows the awesome moves of Lance Mountain and Chris Cook. The other, *Gleaming the Cube*, is a classic. Riders really love this murder mystery. Skateboarding star Stacy Peralta helped make it. The skateboarding scenes are wild. Tony Hawk, Mike McGill, and Rodney Mullen show some unbelievable stunts.

If you want to see the best skateboarders in person, check out the contests held around the globe. The United Skateboarding Association and World Cup Skateboarding both sponsor contests all year round. The United Skateboarding Association has some key events. The Beast of the East, Skate Jam, and the Grand Prix of Skateboarding are all major contests. World Cup Skateboarding has a more worldly feel. They hold the Vans Triple Crown of Skateboarding, the Alp Challenge in Europe, and the South American Championships.

There are also the X Games and the Gravity Games. The X Games started in 1995. The Gravity Games began several years later. Both have **street** and **vert** skateboarding contests. In street, riders wind through a course known as the "funbox." It has rails, steps, and quarter-pipes. Judges score riders based on their technical skill and the difficulty of

From Dogtown to the Bones Brigade

Stacy Peralta was a big name in skateboarding long before *Gleaming the Cube*. In fact, he played a leading role on two of the sport's most famous teams. The first was the Z-Boys, which Stacy joined in the early 1970s. Before contests, the fearsome Z-Boys would boast about their skills. Then they would go out and prove it. The Z-Boys developed their cocky style in "Dogtown," a rough section of Santa Monica, California. When practicing in Dogtown, the Z-Boys always had to watch out for trouble.

After time, the Z-Boys split up. But Stacy was still hungry for competition. In 1979, he got together a new team. The Bones Brigade was sponsored by a company that Stacy started. Ray "Bones" Rodriguez, Alan Gelfand, Rodney Mullen, and Tony Hawk were on the team.

Bob Burnquist performs in the street competition at the 1997 X Games.

the tricks. In the vert category, riders take to the air. They try to nail their best stunts on the half-pipe.

The X Games and the Gravity Games bring in the best skaters. They come from around the world. The competition gets better each year. Thanks to these events, skateboarding has hit the big time.

Skateboarders who compete in vert events perform stunts on a half-pipe, like the one pictured here.

Tony Hawk, shown here rising off a half-pipe, is considered the best skateboarder ever.

Chapter Four

Awesome, Dudes

Skateboarding has had many great stars over the years. Four of these stand out. Tony Alva was the wildest boarder of the 1970s. Rodney Mullen turned freestyle into an art form. Tony Hawk is seen as the best ever. But the future of the sport rides on Bob Burnquist.

Mad Dog

Most people know Tony Alva as "Mad Dog." The nickname suits him perfectly. He was skateboarding's first big star.

Back in the 1970s, Mad Dog was the leader of the Z-Boys. They started an aggressive style of skateboarding. That style has set the tone for many of today's best riders.

Tony spent a lot of time at the beach where he grew up in Santa Monica, California. There, he discovered surfing. With great balance and talent, he was a natural surfer. He also found that his skills served him well on a skateboard.

Tony first tried skateboarding when he was eight. He was already a skilled surfer who could do daring tricks on the waves. His life changed when he realized he could do the same on his skateboard. By age thirteen, Tony was one of the nation's top riders. He and his friends roamed the coast of Southern California in search of empty swimming pools. There, they honed their craft. "We were just trying to emulate our favorite Australian surfers," recalls Tony. "They were doing all this crazy stuff that we were still trying to figure out in the water—but on skateboards, we could do it."

In 1975, after high school, Tony headed for Hawaii. Surfing was still in his blood. Hawaii had the best waves. To make ends meet, Tony posed for skateboard magazines. He also entered local skateboarding contests. It was a great way for him to become known. One day, a Hollywood producer asked him if he wanted to act in a new movie, *Skateboard*. Tony was on his way to becoming a star.

That same year, Tony and some friends entered the Bahne-Cadillac Skateboard Championship in California. They formed their own team, the Z-Boys. The team traveled

Tony Alva flies through the air during a skateboarding stunt.

around the world. No one could beat them. Tony and his friends enjoyed being the best. They dressed in wild clothes. They got wild haircuts. They acted like big shots. "We were pretty hardcore when it came to anybody trying to compete with us," says Tony. "We kind of psyched out everyone before we even started skating against them."

This photo from 1995 shows Tony Alva shredding in a T-shirt from his 1978 movie Skateboard.

In 1977, Tony won the World Pro Championship. That was the first of his three world titles. Mad Dog loved to try out all forms of skateboarding. He once set a world record by jumping over 19 barrels. He liked downhill racing, too.

The business side of skateboarding also interested Tony. He started his own company, Alva Products, in 1977. Soon it became known for making some of the coolest boards. They also made other skateboarding items.

Today, Tony is still involved with the sport. He may be a bit more mellow. But Mad Dog has not lost his edge. "The future is limitless," he says. "Skateboarding can take you as far as your mind and body will let you go."

Perfect, Son

In skateboarding, the end goal is to be perfect. No one knows this better than Rodney Mullen. In a 1986 freestyle contest, he earned his sport's first perfect score. This was no real surprise. Rodney is known as the "King of Freestyle."

Rodney grew up in Florida in the 1970s. When he was eleven, his family moved to Alachua, in the middle of the state. Rodney was not very happy there. The small town was far from any bigger towns or cities. "We had a huge piece of property in the middle of nowhere," he recalls. "No close neighbors, just cows."

That gave Rodney plenty of time to practice. He had bought his first board a year earlier. In no time, Rodney turned into a skilled skateboarder. His greatest talent was freestyle. Creative and smart, he came up with moves no one had ever seen. But he had no interest in competing. He entered his first contest only after friends tricked him into it. When Rodney won, he realized that competition was fun. He entered contests all over the Southeast. Other skateboarders felt they had no chance against him. Soon, the people who held the contests asked him not to enter. He was too good!

Rodney's father also wanted him to stop. He thought his son was wasting his life on the sport. It was time to start thinking about college. Rodney had always been a strong student. His grade point average rarely dipped below a perfect 4.0. But it was clear that Rodney was also an ace on the board. By the time he entered high school, he was the national freestyle champion. This caused a real problem for the teen. Should he listen to his dad and focus on school? Or should he follow his heart and pursue skateboarding?

Though Rodney loved skateboarding, he heeded his father's wishes. He quit the sport after high school and went to college. But it didn't last. He missed skateboarding too much. "It was killing me," he remembers. "It pushed me over the edge. I wrote a long letter telling my dad how much I loved him, but that I couldn't live like this."

Rodney headed for California, where he again found the joy of skateboarding. The sport had more to offer than he ever dreamed. He got roles in movies. He and a friend started a skateboard company. Today, World Industries is one of the biggest skateboard companies around.

Rodney is very busy, and does not compete as much anymore. When he does, he enters street events. There are not very many freestyle competitions anymore. Rodney is one of the best street performers in the country. His freestyle moves fit in well with street moves.

He also has a loyal group of fans. Who is his biggest? His father! "He is really proud," says Rodney. "We don't talk about the old days. We talk about the future."

Simply the Best

Basketball has Michael Jordan. Soccer has Mia Hamm. Skateboarding has Tony Hawk, the "Birdman." There is no debate. Tony is the greatest. "When I skate, I never go halfway," says Tony. "If I don't do my best, it eats at me. It kills me inside."

Hawk developed his killer attitude growing up in Southern California. Born in 1968, he started riding at age nine after his older brother, Steve, gave him a board. Skateboarding soon became Tony's life. He practiced every day for hours on end. "We had to drag him home," recalls his mother, Nancy. "He would kick and scream."

By 1981, Tony was at the top of the sport. For the next 13 years, no one could touch him. Hawk was always a step or two ahead of other skateboarders. He nailed tricks that others never thought of trying. During his career, Tony has invented more than 50 stunts.

Tony Hawk balances with one hand on a rail in midair while skateboarding on a half-pipe.

But even for someone as talented as Tony, raw skill wasn't enough. That is why he looks at 1988 as an important turning point. Tony had already won eight world championships. But he knew he wasn't doing his best. He knew he could reach a new level. For an event in Ohio, Tony set a new goal for himself. Up until that contest, Tony skated mostly by instinct. This time, he practiced hard. He worked on the exact tricks he would do in their exact order. This work paid off. He hit all his tricks, including a 720 (two full turns in the air). After that day, Tony took his riding to an even higher level.

By 1993, Tony had won five more world titles. He decided it was time to stop. He had other goals. He wanted to raise a family. He wanted to start a business. Tony got married in

Tony Hawk skates the half-pipe in Middletown, Rhode Island.

1996. He has three sons, Riley, Spencer, and Keegan. Tony also helped found Birdhouse Projects, a company that makes skateboards.

But the Birdman was born to fly. In 1995, he came out of retirement. At the X Games that year, he took first place in vert. The best was yet to come. In 1999, Tony decided to try a 900 at the X Games. No one had ever done one successfully. The rider had to spin two and a half times in the air. Tony was primed for it. The huge crowd roared in anticipation. Tony's fellow skaters banged their boards on the ground. They wanted to get him pumped. He plunged down one side of the half-pipe and back up the other. He rose and turned once, and then twice. He completed the final half-spin. He landed hard but kept his balance.

Tony had just done the impossible. He had nailed a 900. "This is the best day of my life," he said to his screaming fans. "I couldn't have done it without you. This is the best moment of all time." Skateboarders everywhere agreed.

Burn, Baby, Burn

Before the spring of 1995, no one outside of Brazil had heard of eighteen-year-old Bob Burnquist. He was a quiet guy. But he could certainly ride. At the Slam City Jam in Canada that year, he blew other skaters away. He had an awesome mix of tricks. He finished first in the vert, ahead of Tony Hawk. Since then, no one has forgotten his performance. Bob recalls, "I never thought I'd place well in the contest. It really didn't sink in until a couple of days later. I mean, it was awesome."

Bob was born in Brazil in 1976. His father was from the United States. His mother had lived mostly in South America. Bob and his sister learned to speak English and Portuguese. By his tenth birthday, he was able to speak both languages. This was also when Bob discovered skateboarding. Several years earlier, he had tried surfing. Skateboarding seemed like fun, too. "There were about five of us that hung around," Bob remembers. "We shared the same board."

Bob loved growing up in Brazil. He met interesting people. He learned about other cultures. He played lots of sports, like baseball and mountain biking. Bob also worked on his skateboarding skills. "Skating the hot concrete ramps and hard-to-skate streets of Brazil

Bob Burnquist catches air during the 1999 X Games in San Francisco.

45

gives you an extra edge when you go and skate on a perfect ramp," he says.

One skill Bob nailed was the switch-stance. This is when a skateboarder can ride with either foot forward. It is very hard. For Bob, however, it came easily. "Being in Brazil helped me to not follow the skateboarding norm," he says. "I never had anyone around saying a trick was hard or impossible."

After his big entry in 1995, Bob began touring around the world. Wherever he skated, skaters were in awe of his switch-stance style. In fact, many riders now practice that skill because of Bob. He has plenty of other tricks, too. His most famous is the "Burntwist." "My tricks look spectacular to the outsider's eye, but inside, it's just something I know I can do," he says.

Bob is now a superstar all over the world. Companies pay him to endorse their stuff. He has his own Web site. Fans can read about him and ask him questions. Bob has become a hero to many, especially in Brazil. "I look at it as a mission to pass on a positive word," he says. "I hope I'm doing a good job." Most of all, Bob enjoys the simple fun of skateboarding. "I just have to skate," he says. "I have to be on my board."

Rain Man

Burnquist is concerned about the environment. One of his goals is to save the rain forests in Brazil.

Skateboarding has led to several extreme sports, such as sand boarding.

Chapter Five

Over the Edge

Good skateboarders are skilled athletes. They have great balance and creativity. They are also fearless and will try almost anything. That is one of the great things about skateboarding. It gives you the confidence to be daring. Riders have gone on from there to do other extreme sports.

Long and Fast

The two most popular types of skateboarding are vert and street, but there are others. Longboarding is another form of skateboarding. The name really says it all. A longboard looks just like a skateboard, but is much longer. Some are as long as sixty inches. The wheels on a longboard are also larger and softer. They give a very smooth ride. That's why longboarding is closer to surfing. Some surfers, in fact, use a longboard for practice when they are not in the water.

Downhill is another form of skateboarding. Once again, the name says a lot. In downhill, riders race down steep hills. Along the way, they weave through all sorts of turns. The goal is to finish the run as fast as possible. Downhill was very popular in the 1970s. A rider named John Hutson was probably the best ever. He reached speeds close to sixty miles per hour.

These longboarders are skating down a hill in Northern California.

Street luge is another sport that comes from skateboarding. It is a lot like downhill. But riders lie flat on their backs on special sleds. Their feet face forward. Competitors fly down mountain roads at breakneck speeds. They must wear protective helmets and heavy padding. The sport was first shown at the X Games in 1995. It has become one of the event's most exciting competitions. Michael Sherlock is the greatest champion in street luge history. He has won the most titles and medals.

Snowboarding is a sister sport to skateboarding. This sport first became popular in the early 1970s, many years after the invention of the skateboard. Surfers and skateboarders alike took to snowboarding. It offered many of the same thrills they enjoyed in their sports. They got the same rush of flying through the air. They had the freedom to use their imagination. To this day, surfers snowboard to keep fit during the winter. Many of skateboarding's top stars love the sport, too.

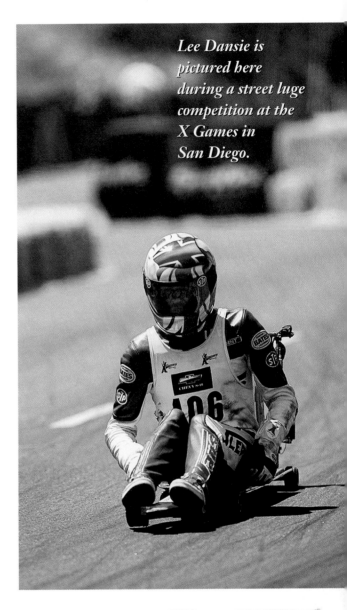

Lee Dansie is pictured here during a street luge competition at the X Games in San Diego.

Speed Demon

Roger Hickey holds the skateboarding speed record at 78.37 mph. He set the mark riding flat on his back on a specially designed board.

Sky surfing, a sport that combines skydiving and surfing, is one of the most extreme sports related to skateboarding.

Anyone who has seen someone **sky surfing** one mile above the earth must ask a question. What's next? The answer is simple. Skateboarders can take their sport anywhere they wish. Who knows? The next Tony Hawk may be living down the street. Or sitting next to you in class. Or even staring back at you in the mirror. As all skateboarders know, if you can dream it, you can do it.

Time Line

3500 B.C.	The wheel is invented in Mesopotamia.
1850 A.D.	Cycling and roller skating gain popularity.
1900	Cars capture the imaginations of adults. Kids continue to use bicycles and roller skates.
1958	Bill Richards and his son, Mark, begin making and selling skateboards.
1963	Brad "Squeak" Blank wins the first skateboarding contest.
1964	Fiberglass skateboards are introduced.
1965	The *Quarterly Skateboarder*, the first magazine devoted to skateboarding, debuts. *Life* magazine publishes its first story on skateboarding. *Skater Dater*, the first movie about skateboarding, premieres. The American Medical Association calls skateboards a "medical menace."
1967	Skateboarding's first wave of popularity dies down.
1969	The snowboard is invented.
1971	Frank Nasworthy introduces the first skateboard with urethane wheels.
1975	The Z-Boys compete together for the first time.
1976	The first skate park opens in Florida.

continued on next page

Time Line *continued*

1977	Willi Winkel invents the half-pipe. Tony Alva wins his first World Pro Championship. Articles on skateboarding appear in *Sports Illustrated* for the first time. Alan Gelfand invents the Ollie.
1978	The movie *Skateboard* is released.
1979	Skateboarding's second wave of popularity dies down. Stacy Peralta forms the Bones Brigade.
1980	Rodney Mullen is crowned national freestyle champion.
1981	*Thrasher* publishes its first issue. Tony Hawk wins his first world title.
1985	Marty McFly, played by Michael J. Fox, "invents" the skateboard in *Back to the Future*.
1989	*Gleaming the Cube* is released.
1995	The X Games debut. Tony Hawk comes out of retirement and wins the vert title at the X Games. Bob Burnquist shocks the skateboarding world by winning the Slam City Jam in Vancouver, Canada.
1999	Tony Hawk performs the first 900 at the X Games. The Gravity Games debut.

Glossary

axles—the steel pieces that connect the wheels to the truck

deck—the board minus the wheels, trucks, and axles

fiberglass—a material, similar to plastic, used to make decks

freestyle—a type of skateboarding competition in which competitors perform stunts such as handstands and wheelies that are scored by a panel of judges

half-pipe—the U-shaped apparatus on which vert stunts are performed

kicktail—the back end of the deck that turns upward

lip—the top edge of a half-pipe or quarter-pipe

mainstream—the most popular aspects of a culture

menace—a threat

nose—the narrow front end of the deck

Ollie—a basic stunt in which the rider and board elevate off the ground and onto or over an object

shredding—another term for skateboarding

sky surfing—a sport that combines skydiving and surfing

street—a type of competition where riders weave through a course with rails, steps, and quarter-pipes and are judged on the accuracy of their skating and difficulty of their stunts

trucks—the pivoting devices that connect the wheels and the axle to the deck

vert—a type of competition where riders perform stunts on the half-pipe that are scored by a panel of judges

wheelie—a basic stunt in which the rider balances on the kicktail and rolls forward without the front wheels touching the ground

To Find Out More

Books

Brooke, Michael. *The Concrete Wave*. Los Angeles, CA: Warwick Publishing, 1999.

Cassorla, Albert. *The Ultimate Skateboard Book*. Philadelphia, PA: Running Press, 1988.

Gutman, Bill. *Skateboarding: To the Extreme!* New York, NY: Tom Doherty Associates, 1997.

Jay, Jackson. *Skateboarding Basics*. Mankato, MN: Capstone Press, 1996.

Werner, Doug. *Skateboarder's Start-Up: A Beginner's Guide to Skateboarding*. Chula Vista, CA: Tracks Publishing, 2000.

Organizations and Online Sites

Grand Prix Skateboarding
http://www.gpskateboarding.com
Official site. Includes information on the Alp Challenge held in Europe.

Skateboard Link
http://www.skateboardlink.com
Offers news, photos, profiles, and a schedule of contests.

United Skateboarding Association
http://www.unitedskate.com
Official site. Includes information on events, membership, and the "skatepark network." Also offers video clips and free stuff.

World Cup Skateboarding
http://www.wcsk8.com
Official site. Includes information on events, results, and products.

A Note on Sources

In researching this book, I tried to draw on as many sources as possible. First, I consulted with another author named Mark Stewart. He knows a lot about sports, and runs his own company called Team Stewart. Mark pointed me in a couple different directions. Then, I visited my local library and searched its database for books written about skateboarding. The most helpful were *The Concrete Wave* by Michael Brooke, *Skateboarding: To the Extreme!* by Bill Gutman, and *The Ultimate Skateboard Book* by Albert Cassorla. Next, I went to a bookstore to learn about magazines for skateboarders. There were five in all: *Transworld Skateboarding, Thrasher, Heckler, Big Brother*, and *Skateboarder*. I called the editor of each publication for advice and "inside" information. Aaron Meza of *Skateboarder* was particularly cooperative. I also found that *ESPN, The Magazine* had a number of good articles. In addition, many newspapers have published interesting features on skateboarding over the years. Finally, I searched the Internet. There, I discovered scores of great sites, including one devoted to ESPN's X Games. It is worth noting that the folks who run the X Games offered whatever assistance they could.

—*Mike Kennedy*

Index

Numbers in *italics* indicate illustrations.

About the Author

Mike Kennedy is a freelance sportswriter whose work has ranged from Super Bowl coverage to historical research and analysis. He has profiled athletes in virtually every sport, including Peyton Manning, Bernie Williams, and Allen Iverson. He is a graduate of Franklin & Marshall College in Lancaster, PA.

Mike has contributed his expertise to other books by Grolier, such as *Auto Racing: A History of Fast Cars and Fearless Drivers*. The other books he authored in this series are *Roller Hockey* and *Soccer*.